ShowTime®

o

Rock 'n Roll

Level 2A
Elementary Playing

This book belongs to: _____

Arranged by

Nancy and Randall Faber

Production Coordinator: Jon Ophoff
Design and Illustration: Terpstra Design, San Francisco
Engraving: Dovetree Productions, Inc.

FABER
PIANO ADVENTURES®
3042 Creek Drive
Ann Arbor, Michigan 48108

A NOTE TO TEACHERS

ShowTime® Piano Rock 'n Roll is a collection of hits from the rock and roll era that is sure to entertain the elementary piano student. The style and rhythmic appeal of the songs make this a great motivational book.

ShowTime® Piano Rock 'n Roll is part of the *ShowTime® Piano* series. "ShowTime" designates Level 2A of the *PreTime® to BigTime® Piano Supplementary Library* arranged by Faber and Faber.

Following are the levels of the supplementary library, which lead from *PreTime®* to *BigTime®*.

PreTime® Piano	(Primer Level)
PlayTime® Piano	(Level 1)
ShowTime® Piano	(Level 2A)
ChordTime® Piano	(Level 2B)
FunTime® Piano	(Level 3A – 3B)
BigTime® Piano	(Level 4)

Each level offers books in a variety of styles, making it possible for the teacher to offer stimulating material for every student. For a complimentary detailed listing, e-mail faber@pianoadventures.com or write us at the mailing address below.

Visit **www.PianoAdventures.com**.

Helpful Hints:

1. Rhythmic continuity can be improved by having the student tap the piece, hands together. (Use the palm or fingertips on the closed fallboard.)

2. Singing the words can add to the enjoyment and helps the student grasp phrasing and rhythm.

3. A circled finger number is used to alert the student to a change of hand position.

About Rock 'n Roll

The beat of rock 'n roll captured the spirit of the youth and the attention of the music industry in the 50s. With its upbeat rhythm, rock 'n roll proved irresistible to all young people.

Pioneers such as Chuck Berry, Fats Domino, and Little Richard led the way for the rock 'n roll king — Elvis Presley. Other greats such as Bill Haley, Carl Perkins, and the legendary Jerry Lee Lewis made significant contributions to the new music form. Bolstered by the rise of celebrity disc jockeys and Dick Clark's "American Bandstand" on television, the sound spread quickly throughout the U.S. and soon to Britain. There it was picked up by The Beatles and The Rolling Stones who, in the 60s, went on to usher in yet another rock era.

ISBN 978-1-61677-632-9

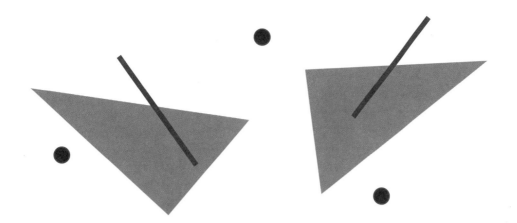

TABLE OF CONTENTS

4

The Loco-Motion

4Words and Music by
GERRY GOFFIN and CAROLE KING

(prepare R.H.)

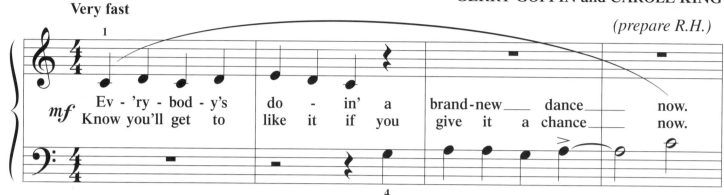

Ev - 'ry - bod - y's do - in' a brand-new dance now.
Know you'll get to like it if you give it a chance now.

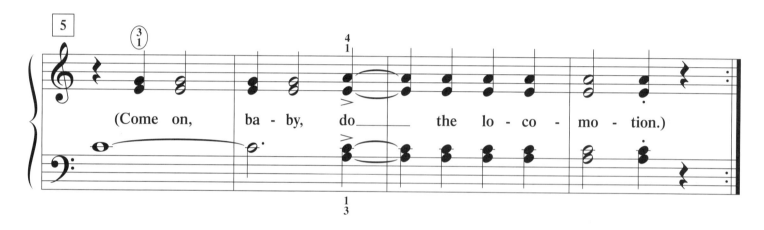

(Come on, ba - by, do the lo - co - mo - tion.)

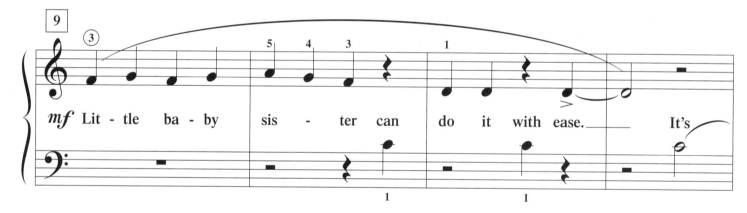

Lit - tle ba - by sis - ter can do it with ease. It's

Teacher Duet: (Student plays 1 octave higher)

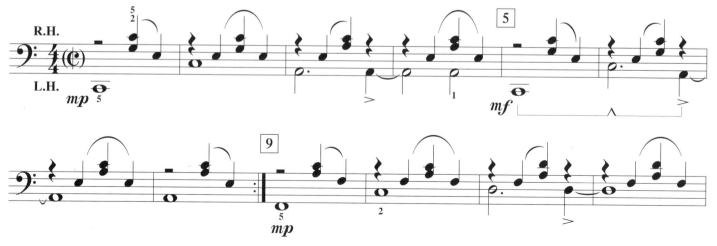

444444444

4

5

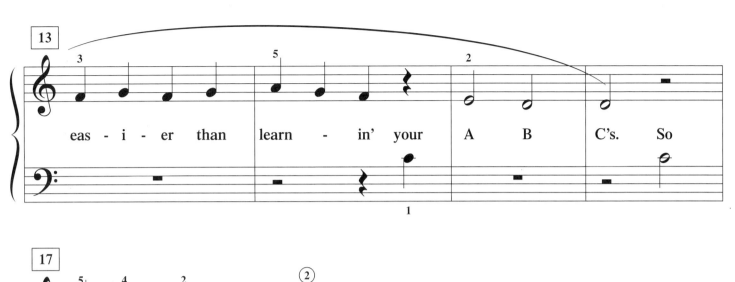

easier than learnin' your A B C's. So

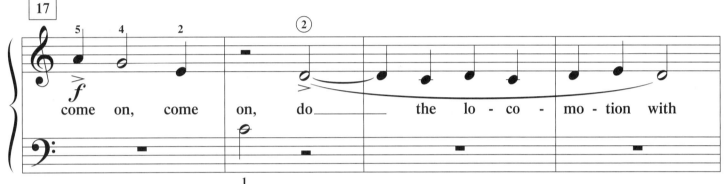

come on, come on, do the loco-motion with

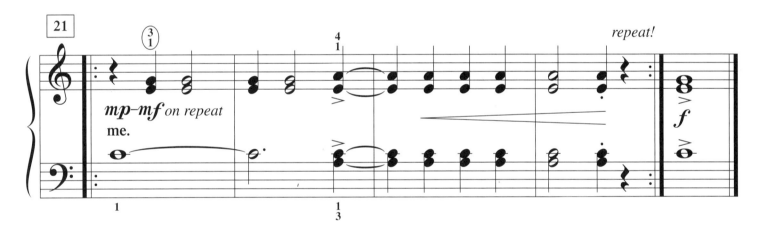

me.

mp–mf on repeat

repeat!

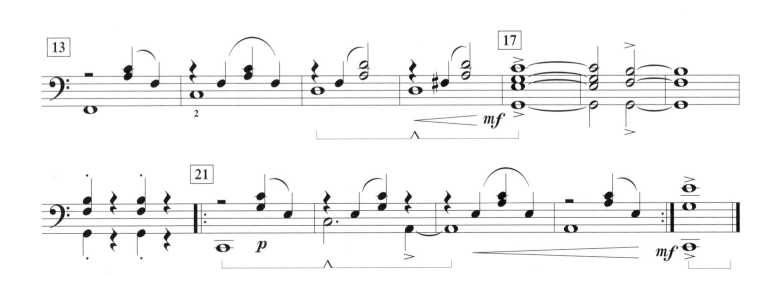

FF3008

A Groovy Kind of Love

Words and Music by TONI WINE
and CAROLE BAYER SAGER

Rather slowly

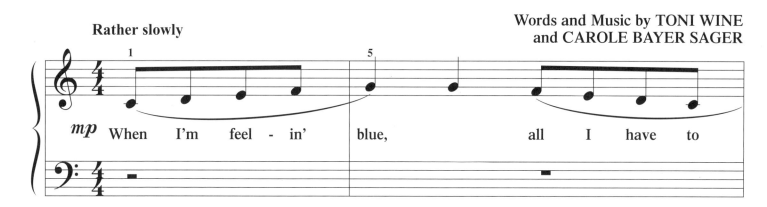

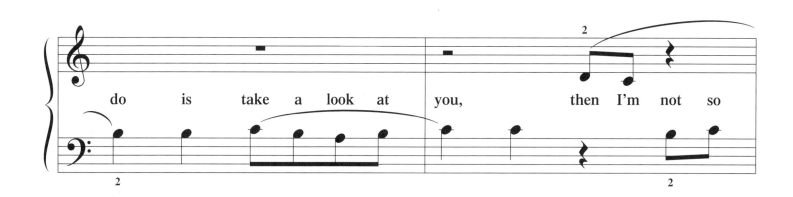

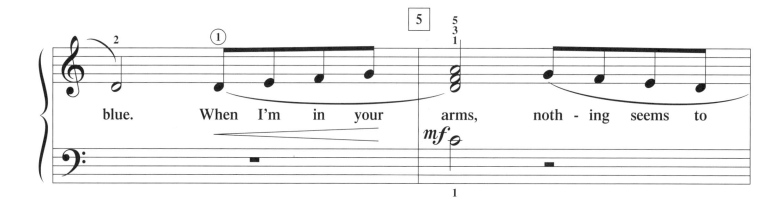

Teacher Duet: (Student plays 1 octave higher)

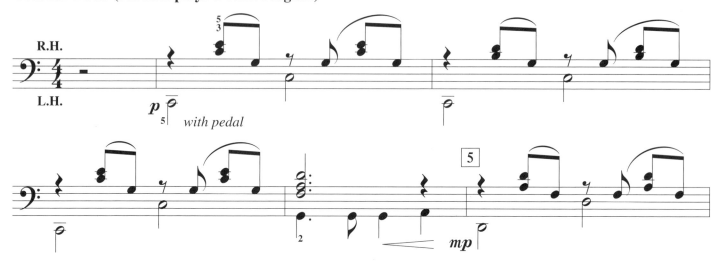

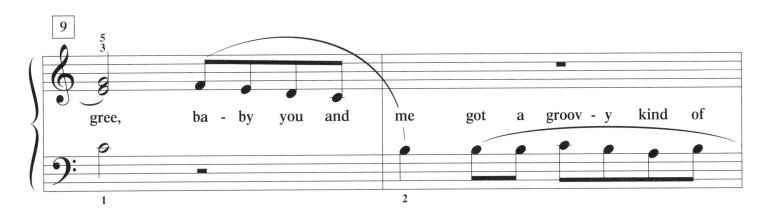

FF3008

Lollipop

Words and Music by
BEVERLY ROSS and JULIUS DIXON

Cheerful Rock swing*

Swing the 8th notes!

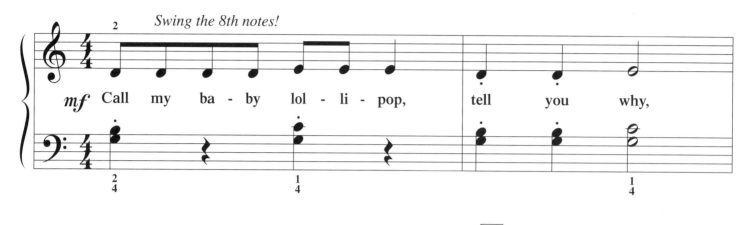

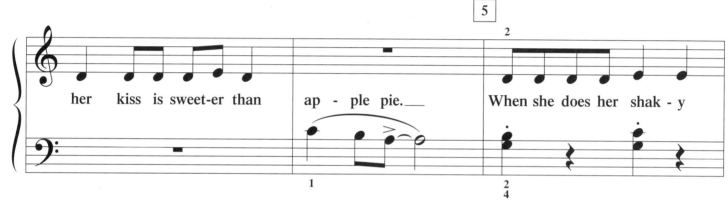

*Note to Teacher: Eighth notes in student and teacher part may
be played in a long-short "swing" pattern.

Teacher Duet: (Student plays 1 octave higher)

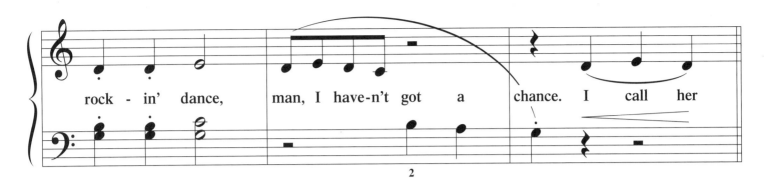

rock - in' dance, man, I have-n't got a chance. I call her

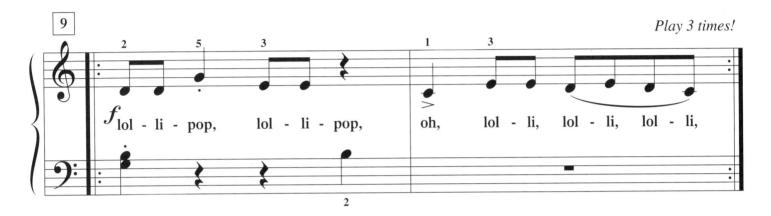

Play 3 times!

9

f lol - li - pop, lol - li - pop, oh, lol - li, lol - li, lol - li,

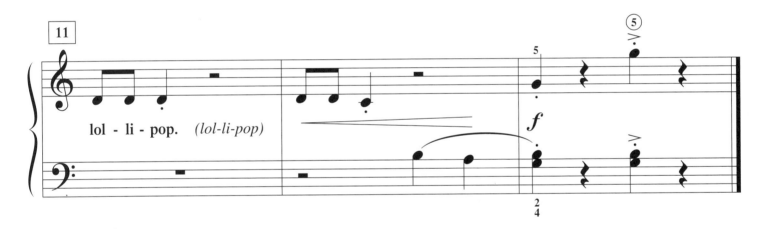

11

lol - li - pop. *(lol-li-pop)*

Play 3 times! **11**

9

10

Baby Elephant Walk

from the Paramount Picture *HATARI!*

By HENRY MANCINI

2 measures rest when
student plays with duet.

Moving along happily

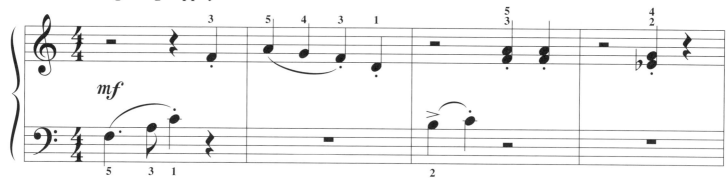

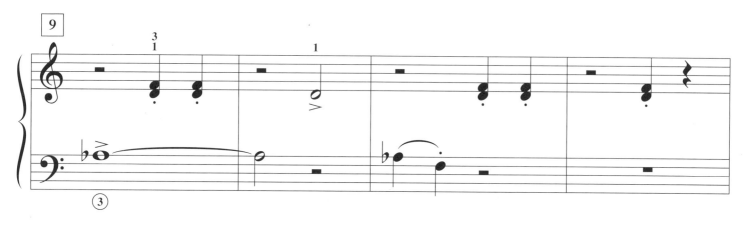

Teacher Duet: (Student plays 1 octave higher)

At the Hop

Words and Music by ARTHUR SINGER,
JOHN MADARA, and DAVID WHITE

With a solid beat

Let's go to the hop!

Let's go to the hop!

Let's go to the hop!

Let's go to the

Teacher Duet: (Student plays as written)

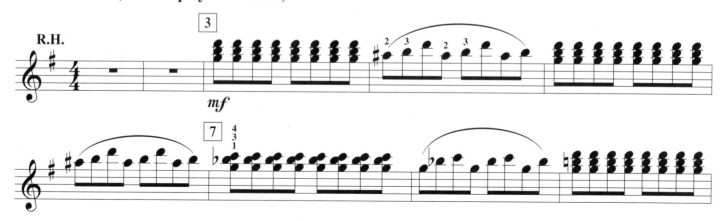

R.H.

hop!

Let's go to the hop!

Come on, let's go to the

hop!

Let's go to the hop!

Ain't No Mountain High Enough

Words and Music by
NICKOLAS ASHFORD and VALERIE SIMPSON

Rather slowly, with soul

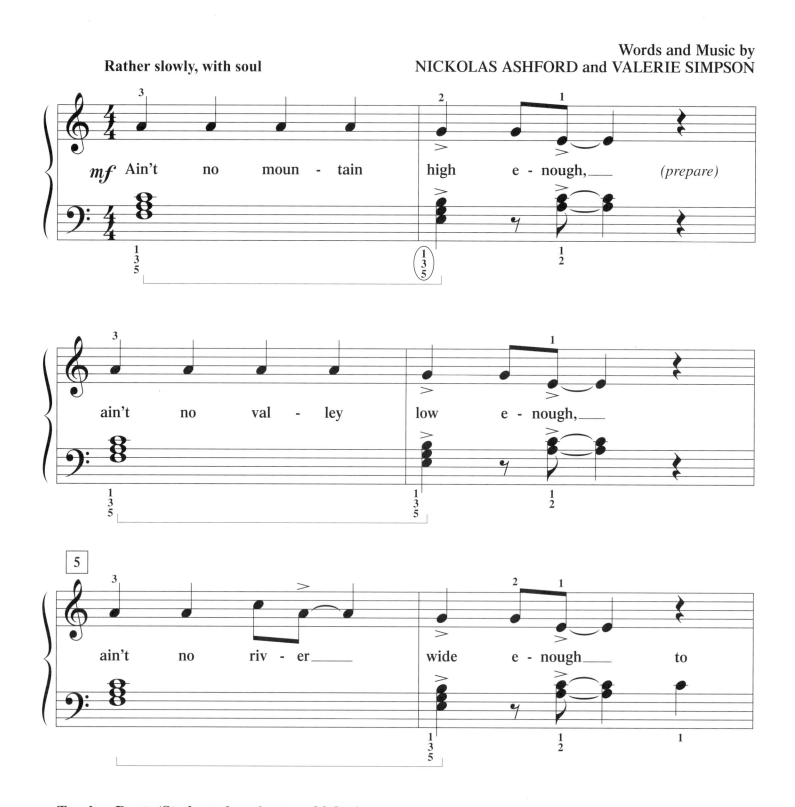

Teacher Duet: (Student plays 1 octave higher)

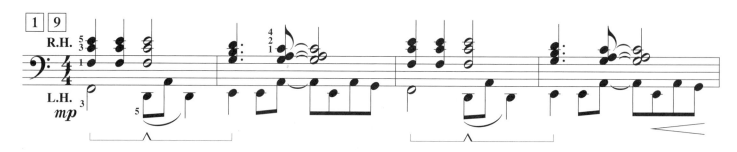

Yakety Yak

Words and Music by
JERRY LEIBER and **MIKE STOLLER**

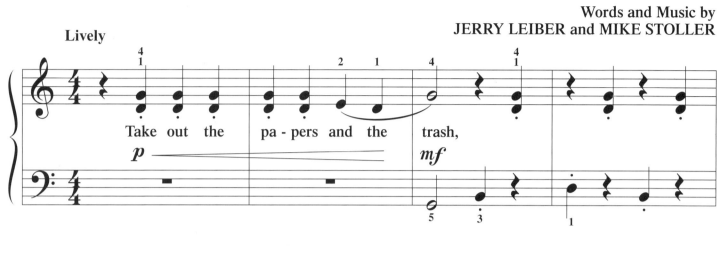

Take out the pa - pers and the trash,

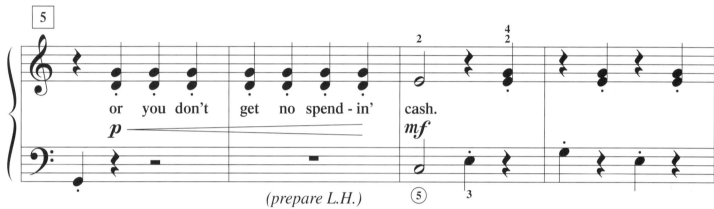

or you don't get no spend - in' cash. *(prepare L.H.)*

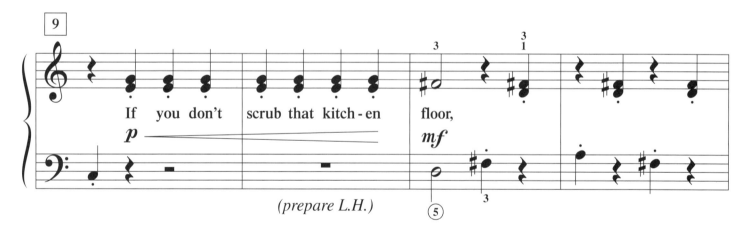

If you don't scrub that kitch - en floor, *(prepare L.H.)*

you ain't gonna rock and roll no more. Yak-et - y yak. *(Don't talk* *(prepare R.H.)*

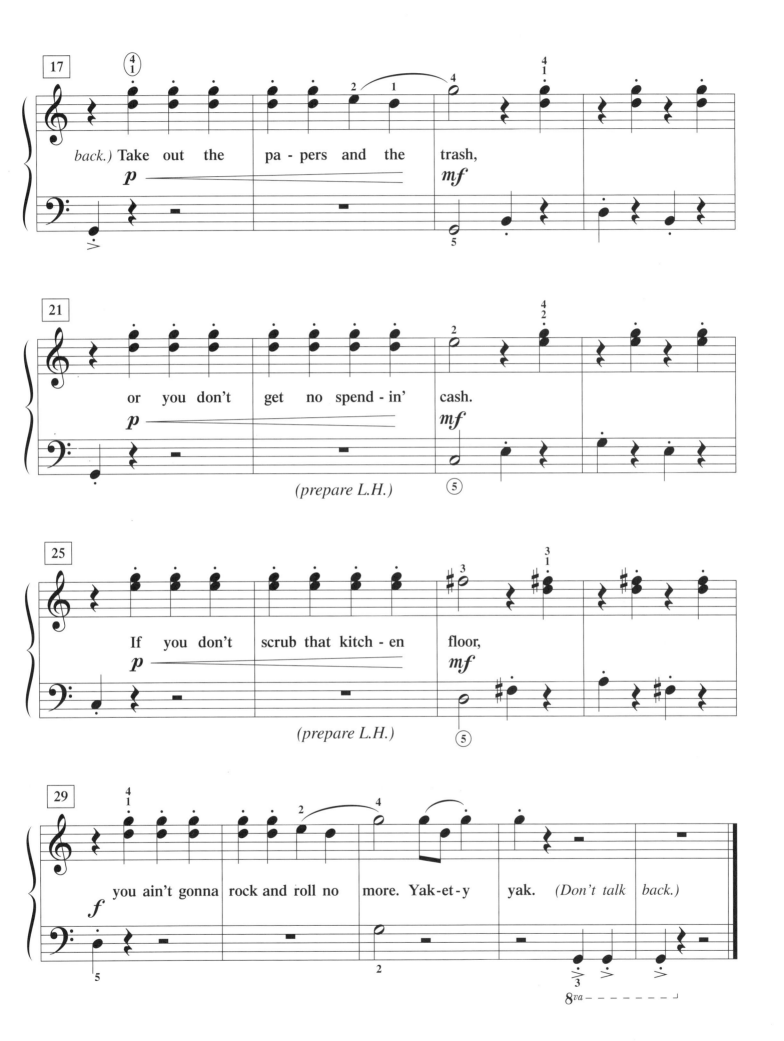

18

Lava Lamp

Music by
NANCY FABER

Flowing freely

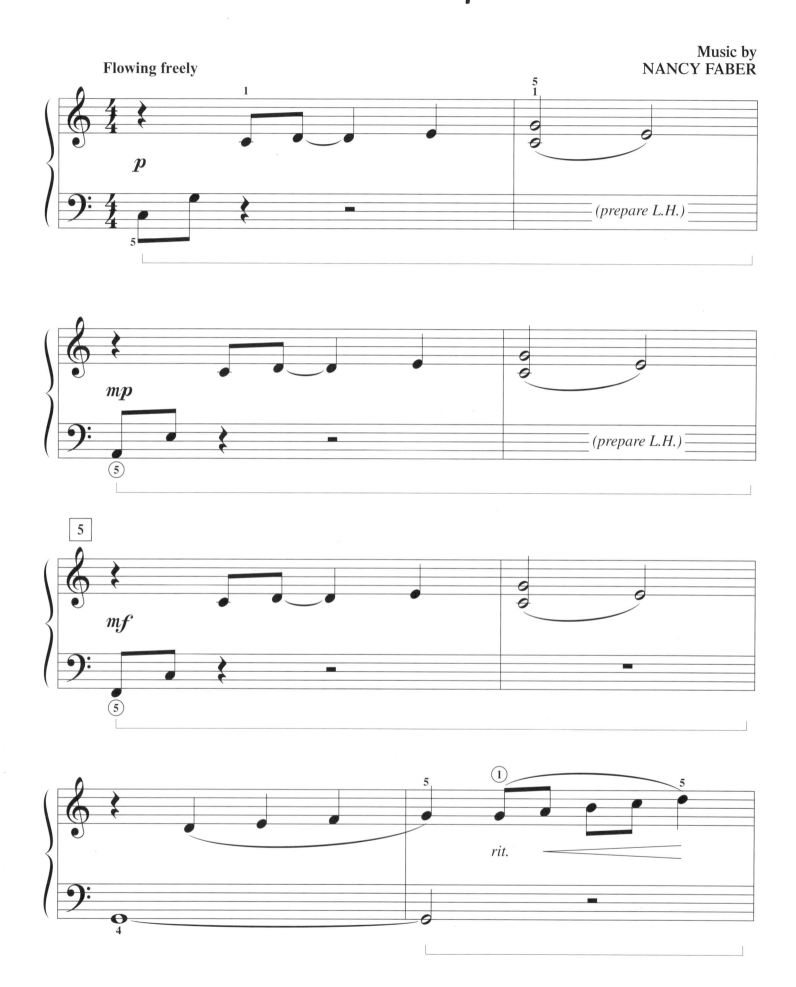

Copyright © 2012 Dovetree Productions, Inc. c/o FABER PIANO ADVENTURES.
International Copyright Secured.   All Rights Reserved.

FF3008

19

FF3008

Undercover Rock

**Music by
JON OPHOFF**

21

Teacher Duet: (Student plays as written)

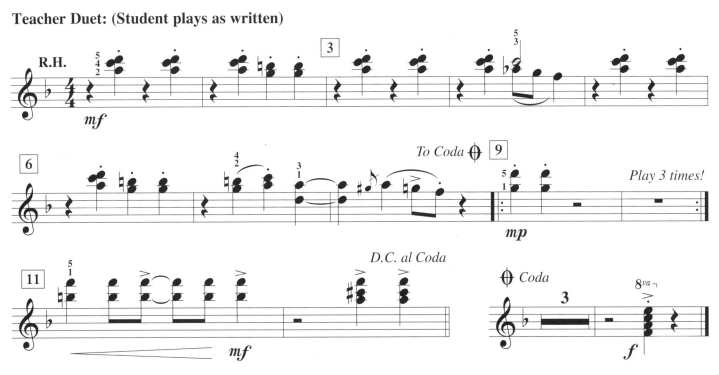

FF3008

Twist and Shout

4 measures rest when
student plays with duet.

Words and Music by
BERT RUSSELL and PHIL MEDLEY

Teacher Duet: (Student plays 1 octave higher)

24

Just like I knew   you   would.   (Knew you would.)